THE FIFTH DIMENSION

Derek + Barbara

Thank you for played &
fellowship —

Phil

The Fifth Dimension

PHIL BOOTH

KINGSWAY PUBLICATIONS
EASTBOURNE

Biblical quotations are from the
New International Version © International Bible Society
1973, 1978, 1984
Published by Hodder & Stoughton

Front cover photo: The Image Bank

British Library Cataloguing in Publication Data

Booth, Phil
    The fifth dimension.
    1. Christian life
    I. Title
    248.4

    ISBN 0-86065-714-0

Production and printing in Great Britain for
KINGSWAY PUBLICATIONS LTD
Lottbridge Drove, Eastbourne, E Sussex BN23 6NT by
Nuprint Ltd, Harpenden, Herts AL5 4SE

To the memory of Miriam ('Mim') Booth
who knew the life in the Spirit which
is explored in this book. It was she
who wrote:
'The greatest enemy of the work of God
is the work for God.'

Contents

	Foreword	9
	Introduction	11
1	The Edge of Knowing	15
2	The Eternity of Now	19
3	Those Who Live in the Eternity of God	23
4	Characteristics of the New Creation	27
5	The Glorious Weakness of the New Creation	33
6	Guidance for the New Creation	37
7	Operating from Rest	43
8	Activity of the Living Christ	47
9	'Learn of Me'	53
10	The Home-Ground of the New Creation	55
11	The Inner Revelation of Christ	59
12	The Fight from Rest	65
13	Acceptable Failures	71
14	Much Closer Than a Brother	75

15	God, A Consuming Fire . . .	79
16	. . . Or God as Cool Light	83
17	The Enemy of Rest	87
18	Priorities of the Fifth Dimension	91
19	Believing—or Knowing?	95
20	A Different Kind of Person	99
21	Resurrection Life—For Others	103
22	And Now Forward?	107
23	An Outline of Action	113
	A Prayer	117
	Bibliography	119

Foreword

Phil Booth's book fascinates me.

He presents *faith* as the sixth sense that relates us to God, as the other five senses relate us to the world. And so *timelessness* is the Fifth Dimension, which enables us to perceive from God's viewpoint and understand with his mind all events and occurrences in our daily lives. The other four dimensions enable us to perceive and understand from a merely human angle, but it is the Fifth Dimension which is all important.

Phil leads us step by step along a narrow pathway called 'REST'. Sometimes the way may not seem very clear, the pathway partially concealed in the mysterious explanations: and one has to follow closely, if one is not to slip off into the bogland mire on either side. This mire is 'STRIVING'—striving to understand, striving to do something, striving against doubts and anxieties, even striving to achieve and maintain the desired rest!

One must realise that the famous words of Galations 2:20, 'I am (have been) crucified with Christ: nevertheless I live; yet not I, but Christ lives in me, and the life that I now live, I live by the faith of the Son of God who loved me and gave himself for me' were written by Paul to *babes* in Christ. These were young converts from Judaism and paganism, who had no New Testament to read, and who had only heard a minimum of teaching from Paul on his few brief visits during three missionary journeys over twelve years. Therefore one *must* seek to enter into and appropriate the verse's truth and its rest, rather than relegate it to some mystical experience of a few mature super-saints.

May the Lord himself give us his understanding by the power of his indwelling Holy Spirit, and fill us with a veritable hunger and thirst after righteousness. May we each one be prepared to be yoked to our Lord and Master, that we may enter into his promised *rest*, as we learn of him.

Thankyou, Phil, for challenging us to move into this Fifth Dimension in our daily Christian lives, and so to enjoy the reality of REST as we sit with God in heavenly places and watch him at work in his world, accepting the honoured privilege of being his co-labourers. Thankyou as you lead us steadily through the moorland mists, out into the cool light of God's glorious heavenlies, and away from the consuming fire of his wrathful judgements.

Helen Roseveare

Introduction

Halfway through this book, I had to stop and go back to this point again! I suddenly realised that I was handling a boomerang which at that moment was not hitting the target, but returning and hitting me!

Some African friends of mine once showed me that when you point the finger at anyone, there are three fingers pointing back at yourself. I was not intentionally pointing the finger at anyone. But if what I was writing was intended to 'edify and enlighten' you, then I was inferring that you needed something which I had to offer. I saw three fingers pointing back at me very very clearly. Two different metaphors, but whether boomerang or fingers, I had to go back in thought for some years and examine what I would call my Christian service in the light of what I was writing. It was a very illuminating exercise!

But among others, there was one thing I did learn from this which was invaluable to me. I found out how to deal with anything that God showed me to be religious junk. It was all very well to examine, to challenge if you like, all that I had sought to do in Christian life and service, but I could not put the clock back, nor could I press on without straightening things out. What was the use of carrying a load of 'wood, hay and stubble' (as the apostle Paul described it) when what I wanted, and what God required, was 'gold, silver and precious stones'? Not everything was to be rejected, by the grace of God. But here and there . . .!

It was all very simple, really. Repentance was at the heart of the matter. Just as if I was being converted once again! 'Sorry, Lord. I had the temerity to offer you my own self-satisfying religious activity. Please forgive me, and clean it away.'

And he did!

So, now I can get on with the job. If you happen to discover as we go along together something similar to what I did, then you will know how to deal with the matter.

Bible-believing Christians tend to have one unexpected limitation to full, enjoyable, Christian spiritual living. It is the Bible! Immediately, I must add something perhaps more acceptable at the moment. I would say that we can have a loyalty to the written 'Word of God' which is so strong that it works against the full experience and enjoyment of union with the living 'Word of God'.

'The letter kills, but the Spirit gives life' declares Paul boldly (2 Cor 3:6). This, and the testimony of many Christian mystics since his day, would suggest that beyond the edge of the written words of Christian Scripture there is a quality of life to be lived which is directly related to, but not verbally defined by, the words on the page.

Most Christians will have sung at some time or other the devotional hymn written by Mary Rathbury. Perhaps unthinkingly to some extent, we have sung, 'Beyond the sacred page, we seek Thee Lord'.

Precisely.

'My thoughts are not your thoughts, neither are my ways your ways' declared the Lord (Is 55:8), and adds that the difference is as great as the distance between the earth and the heavens. Notice that this difference relates to 'thoughts' as well as to 'ways' . . . Yet I believe that God does reveal his thoughts and his ways by the Holy Spirit to those who will receive them. Our Lord Jesus called on those who had ears to hear, to hear. There must be something of special readiness about such ears!

I believe that we miss the revelation of the 'mystery of God' quite often by an unwillingness to follow through logically the statements which are written. To avoid the radical and hard-to-accept truth that is stated, there is a tendency to isolate the words and put on them a possibly correct alternative translation (presenting a truth but not the whole truth) when a logical and at least equally correct one would lead us to a wonderfully new kind of life. We shall examine examples of this later. But this deeper truth can be disturbing to an established position, even though we accept that

'My thoughts are not your thoughts by the distance of the earth from the heavens'. And how we hate to be disturbed—even by God!

If ever I understand God fully in this life he will have become unsatisfactory. But it seems that he encourages us to seek to know him and understand him more and more. And he who gives life is Spirit, and is always looking for those who will worship him in Spirit as well as in truth. In truth—but just a little beyond the humanly understood and written word—in Spirit as well. There is a Fifth Dimension. And it is intended to be available to us all.

I

The Edge of Knowing

We cannot profitably share all our thoughts to the
end of their development with everybody. With
many there comes a point past which they will not
go. There is an emphasis which they cannot accept.
'Heresy' is but the over-emphasis of a truth beyond
a balance according to their thinking. There are
concepts which—to be frank—stretch their minds
beyond normal understanding. I am one of those
people. It is here that we are dependent on revelation, and not everybody knows the Holy Spirit in a
personal sense so that he can exercise his ministry
in this way. None of this is intended to be conde-
scending, although it sounds like it. I would suggest that it is a statement of fact that we can all
recognise.

For many years in the past it was my privilege to
speak in a number of Bible Colleges. I was invited
to address the students (and sometimes the staff!).
So long as my material was of a devotional character, the topic was left to me. Although I hope that I

always spoke as guided by God, it is also true that the degree of liberty I had to 'speak my heart' varied considerably from College to College. Often there was a straight-down-the-line orthodoxy which almost forbad even the use of phraseology which was not 'biblical'. But there were the wonderful exceptions where a visitor like myself could fly some wonderful 'kites' when it was clear that the string was anchored in the Word. I would speak openly and with a smile of my 'heresies'. The beauty of such situations was that we shared real spiritual food together, and afterwards could say 'It was good for us to be here.' In passing, it has been encouraging in after years to meet people who still remember those times with gratitude to God for an expanded vision, a deeper if undefinable life in the Spirit which has stood the test of time.

At such places, the time-table rarely indicated the topic for consideration. I found it difficult to define it often, anyhow. And I would now. The nearest one can get is 'Experiential Theology', and by that we must understand that I have a hobby horse. Theology should wear boots. It is something not only for the ivory tower, but also for the stone-floored kitchen. Furthermore, although perfection of experience is not of this world, it is necessary that this 'experiential theology' should at least be in part personal experience. If only head knowledge is shared, there is no life in it. This is well in line with Paul's great declaration of his life's purpose—to know Christ, and the power of his resurrection, and to have fellowship with him in his death so that he might attain to the resurrection from that death. (Phil 3:10). To which he adds that he has not yet fully attained this truth, but that he presses on in order to do so.

Illustrative of the very thrust of truth to which I am alluding, it will be realised that Paul is not here referring to the resurrection of the dead as we normally speak of it. That, surely, is something everyone reaches without any effort! That seems clear from Rev 20:11–13, ('. . . the dead, great and small . . . each person judged . . .') and from our Lord's reference to the eventual judgement of the 'sheep and the goats'. No. The 'death' here is that which enters the life of the believer in the will of God and which becomes the 'taking up of the cross' to which our Lord referred. Die there, and the resurrection from that death will lead to fuller life and new dimensions even as it did in the experience of the Lord Jesus. The vision of that had captured Paul as it has done many since. No wonder everything else was as rubbish.

Here is the edge of a new dimension of life. We are familiar with three—height, length, breadth,—because the world in which we live is obviously that. It is valid to add one other also, that of time. If there should be a creation which is but a second behind us in its expression, then we are completely unconscious of it! But you and I exist in the continuing 'now' of our experience.

'Now is the day of salvation' we say. But that 'now' is related immediately to the three-dimensional world in which we live. 'Now' is the only time dimension shared with all. The hour of the day and the season of the year varies in different parts of the world. I can speak on the telephone to a friend in Australia and tell him we are having a hot summer. He growls back that it is a perishing cold winter! Similarly, I tell my friend in New York that I am about to have lunch at noon. He yawns, and says his breakfast is about ready at 7am. But we all—every one of us—say it is NOW.

And yet, beyond this even, we see the glimmer of a Fifth Dimension. But clearly it must be related to the more usually accepted four.

2

The Eternity of Now

God is said to 'inhabit eternity' (Is 57:15), or he 'lives for ever' as another translation puts it. We would expect no less. But as soon as we realise what 'eternity' and 'for ever' implies we are more in the realm of 'concepts' than is comfortable for those who are satisfied with words alone. For instance, 'for ever' and even 'eternity' are thought of as being from now into the future. In other words, we are now living in some previous person's 'for ever'! That is true, of course, and it is a part of our own 'for ever'. 'Eternity past' is even more beyond our mental grasp than 'eternity future'.

To avoid verbal awkwardness, I want to use the word 'eternity'—old fashioned though it may be in the eyes of some—to express this 'for ever'. Then we can say truthfully that eternity is not a form of endless time. It is not that, even if we think of 'eternity past' as well and eternity now and future. Eternity is a never-ceasing *now*. How beautiful it is, therefore, that the one who revealed himself as the ever-present-tense Person—the I AM—should be said to rest in, dwell, inhabit, tabernacle (Heb: *shaken*) eternity. He is the only one who could!

It would seem, therefore, that time began when the I AM of eternity (the ever *now*) created something material in addition to spiritual. 'In the beginning, God created . . .' (Gen 1:1). That was the beginning of time as we know it. What I add could be called sheer assumption. But if we cannot accept the idea that this God, the I AM, would create something that was formless and empty and surrounded by darkness, then we may well be touching the secret behind the first two verses of Genesis chapter one and the subsequent verses of that chapter.

Other things begin to fall into place. The Lord Jesus speaks of the King saying to the redeemed 'Take your inheritance, the kingdom prepared for you since the creation of the world'. (Mt 25:34). We are, rather obviously, 'creatures of time'. But of the Lord Jesus we read that he *is* slain 'from the foundation of the world' (Rev 13:8). Even more wonderfully, it is stated 'For he chose us in him (Christ) *before* the creation of the world.' That, of course, is the truth from the human or created being's point of view. Although the truth from God's point of view may appear to be mere playing with words, the fact is that before creation, since creation and forward to the final consummation of God's purposes—they are all the same in relation to time to the I AM, the one who lives in the never ceasing now.

Our various schools of theology are by definition different attempts to explain and to study God. Inevitably, they must be from a human point of view. While that means that there must be different viewpoints, the fact remains that the semantically inexplicable I AM who is alive in the eternal 'now' can be known experientially through Jesus Christ who has revealed him. Our known union with him can deliver us from the bounds—one could say bondage—of the three dimensional, time-controlled, human form of living. This latter can be very wonderful in many ways. It is intended so. But without leaving it behind for the time being, we are called and exhorted by Scripture to live it in direct relationship with the kingdom of the eternal now. We are provoked to start living now, increasingly, the quality of life and the effectiveness of life which is proceeding from him. This can only mean living by new criteria which are valid in a new dimension which is rooted in the scriptural revelation of the I AM and our union with him.

3

Those Who Live in the Eternity of God

This dimension of the 'eternal now' which I have called the Fifth Dimension would appear at first sight to be quite outside the possibility of human experience. In fact, this is true, unless there is first some radical dealing with him who 'inhabits eternity'. But the God-intended possibility of a human entering into that experience is another thing. A change of being is necessary; one must become something different—a different creation. But it is possible. This New Creation must live—or learn to live—not only by the ethics and morals of the kingdom of God, but also by the points of reference which are relevant in a totally new world. No longer is it a matter of mental reason, touch, sight, smell, hearing, taste and time. While these functions will be in our experience just as they were with the Lord Jesus Christ, nevertheless they will no longer be the basis or criteria from which we consciously and unconsciously make the large and small decisions which enable us to live.

In the Gospel according to St John we find in chapter three the conversation that the Lord Jesus had with the sincere but mystified Nicodemus. The central thing that he had to see at first was that humanity could only produce humanity.

'That which is born of flesh is flesh.' But natural birth could not produce anyone who could even see the kingdom of God. There had to be a new birth—another birth—a birth by the Spirit from 'above'. 'That which is born of the Spirit is Spirit.'

As John testifies (Jn 1:12–13) 'To all who received him, to those who believed in His name,' (Jesus—Saviour) 'He gave the right to become children of God—born of God.' In the end, we have to admit that true Christians are not just ordinary human beings, even if some of them try to live as if they were. This has little to do with morals, ethics, or anything in such realms. At the heart of things we are talking about a different kind of being. Such beings do have a reasonably defined level of morals, ethics and general conduct. But merely observing such manner of living will not make one a Christian. Dolefully scratching its head or suckling its child will never make an ape a human being . . . in spite of certain mutual resemblances. It is a different creation—wonderful maybe, but different. A human being is different from a Christian—wonderful no doubt, but different. Human beings and apes can well be accepted as being created by God; but the true Christian is born of God. He is a new and different creation. And many of his problems arise from

24

ignoring that fact, and therefore seeking to live by the same principles as the good, moral, ethical human being which he now sees as infinitely important. But unfortunately, even as a Christian, he finds that his personal efforts are of little use.

Inevitably, there are eternal issues involved in all of this. The human bodies of both human beings and Christians die. And it is at that point in time that the difference between the two creations becomes vividly revealed as they enter the eternal NOW. But this Fifth Dimension need not be at all strange to the one who is born of God, the new creation. It can be the domain in which he has been living already to a large extent. But we must examine both the nature of this New Creation as well as his true and native environment in which he can have the privilege—and should take it—of living day by day. This could all be considered 'Sunday school stuff'. This is true—it is to be revealed to babes! (Mt 21:16). But the implications can challenge the most mature adult.

4

Characteristics of the New Creation

'Christ in all the Scriptures' is an excellent line of study, even if it becomes a little difficult at times. But 'Christ in all experience' must be our aim once we have realised the truth of Colossians 3:4, 'Christ . . . our life'. There are, of course, other passages such as Galatians 2:20 which convey the same truth: 'I live, yet not I, but Christ.' Not a life changed, but a life exchanged—mine for his. This must not be confused with the excellent sentiment of dedication to him: '100% sold out for God'. This may well be a marvellous and worthy action on the part of a child of God. But we are looking at something more, much more, wonderful. We are facing something that *God* does when we become a New Creation. He becomes our life. What appears to be our living a 'normal' life can be really him living his life through our bodies. There is always something about such a 'normal' human being! It is a bush which is burning but not consumed . . . (Ex 3:3). And people still 'turn aside' to enquire why; what is it that is different?

It is the New Creation which is indwelt by Christ. The 'old creation' could be indwelt by nothing or by 'many devils' (Mt 12:43–45). And, indeed, our human bodies which are still subject to death, and whose redemption is only potential at the present time, can be still activated by evil spirits. But that New Creation, where Christ dwells, is unassailable, because Christ conquered Satan himself when he died on the cross at Calvary (Col 2:13–15). Jesus Christ was the 'last Adam' (1 Cor 15:45) and when he died and came alive again it meant that the old Adamic race could cease to exist. The last Adam had died. A New Creation race had begun. But we would not have it so and the two races exist side by side to this day. Each race has two 'consciousnesses' (not two 'natures'). The New Creation can still 'hear' the devil and also God (just as the Lord Jesus could, and the newly created Adam of Genesis), and the old creation can 'hear' the devil and also God in his conscience (at least for a time) as the Saviour gives a measure of light as he seeks to make his love and grace known.

But one of the first things we have to learn is that the New Creation is as weak in itself as was the old creation. This is sometimes hard to admit until we accept that we cannot live the Christian life as we ought. We know what God wants, but we cannot do it. We know what God does not want, and yet we often do just that thing. Only the fact that we are born of the Spirit enables us to know from the heart what God requires. But to do that is another thing! (Rom 7:15–22).

God will allow even failure in order to teach us that he alone can live the life we hope to experience. We learn to welcome anything which makes us consciously more dependent on God; more consciously weak; and therefore more consciously relying on the I AM to live his life through us. Paul declared 'When I am (consciously) weak, then am I strong' (2 Cor 12:10). I am emphasising 'consciously'. This is no mere theological statement of the obvious. Nor is it a sentimental and self-excusing let-out. Few of us enjoy the experience of the kind of weakness of which I write. And yet it is a further step at the beginning of the way into the Fifth Dimension.

The ultimate weakness is death, which leads eventually to the ultimate strength which is resurrection; strength, that is, in that the resurrection body is undying no matter where it finds itself. At last, some say, we are at rest. That obviously relates to the physical world—the world of four dimensions. But whoever we are, the person who has left the body is anything but at rest. We must look at this fact later on. Meanwhile, the whole of the fourth chapter of the Letter to the Hebrews exhorts us to enter into a spiritual rest, an inner rest, *now* in this life. In a similar way, our Lord invites us to the same spiritual rest, 'Take my yoke (the one I am wearing) upon you, and you will learn from me, and find rest for your souls' (Mt 11:29). Do not go on labouring! As the fourth chapter of the Letter to the Hebrews points out (v 12) the discernment of God differentiates between the soul (human endeavour) and the spirit (that which God does through us). It judges between the bones (outer form) and the marrow (where the life is).

Perhaps this is the appropriate time in our thinking when we should face a fact that I have found very thought-provoking. Paul points out that in the Christian life a foundation has been laid—the Lord Jesus Himself (1 Cor 3:10–11). But then he goes on to exhort us very solemnly to be careful how we build on that foundation. Will it be 'gold, silver, precious stones' or 'wood, hay, stubble'? If I have learned to operate from rest then the Holy Spirit will have built through me in 'gold, silver, precious stones'. But if I have laboured myself, then I shall have built in 'wood, hay and stubble'. Paul says bluntly that such 'works' will be burnt up in the testing fire of God. On one occasion, Paul speaks of himself as 'labouring more abundantly than them all', but quickly adds, 'Yet not I but the grace of God which was with me.' (1 Cor 15:10).

A deeply respected friend of mine has found this truth difficult to accept. 'If a young child brings home from school' she argues 'some simple model he has made from odds and ends, it may well be just recognisable for what he intends it to be. He has done his best. In love, Mother and Father will accept it without criticism and will embrace it and the child in their love. Will not my heavenly Father do similarly in his love in spite of the imperfections of my efforts? Does he not look upon the heart?' I know the human experience well; I still treasure my six-year old's 'Book of my Life'! But in the world of publishing it has no place even though he himself continued in my love as my child!

We are in danger of missing the point. The motive is not in question. And we shall still be saved 'as by fire' (1 Cor 3:15). But it is the nature of the material which is in question. Some can go through fire without being destroyed, and some cannot. Humanity—good, well motivated humanity—can only produce things which can live in this four dimensional world. It is those created out of the Fifth Dimension which can stand the testing 'as by fire'. Someone has said 'May we have much to lay at the Saviour's feet.' We understand what he means. And therefore we must learn to live and work out of the Fifth Dimension. Already we have seen that this means an acceptance of a total weakness before God—and sometimes before men and women. We learn to maintain a 'rest' which is the enjoyment of a union with him who is the eternal I AM.

5

The Glorious Weakness of the New Creation

We have established from the Bible several important characteristics of the New Creation. It is necessary in everyday life to remind ourselves of these
from time to time; a brief summary is not out of
place here therefore.

This new being which takes over our bodies in
place of our human selves is something which is
created by God at a specific point in time. The
potential for this has always existed even before
time began. Expressed from the human point of
view it is that 'God has from the beginning chosen
you to salvation' (2 Thess 2:13 et alia). But 'he has
chosen us in him (Jesus Christ) before the foundation of the earth.' The New Creation is vested in
the I AM. The advent (I use the word deliberately
because Christ comes to live in my body) of the
New Creation comes into human experience
because the last Adam has died and the new race
begun with his resurrection. And 'to those who
receive him, he gives the right to become children

of God—children born not of natural descent . . . but born of God' (Jn 1:12–13). As the Lord Jesus pointed out himself, 'Flesh gives birth to flesh, but the Spirit gives birth to spirit.' (Jn 3:6). In human terms, we are born again from above and become a new living spiritual creation. Of course, this New Creation is recognisable as being related to the old one—the risen Christ could be seen as the one who had walked with his disciples. But there is something which is gloriously different, something which can be seen but which is inexplicable; apart from saying that the person is somehow different. No more true word was ever spoken!

I do not think we can explain just how this happens, but millions of people know this experience, even though the full implications of it may not yet have been realised. The process of realisation is what is normally called spiritual growth. This should go on throughout all of life, because obviously God is much bigger than even the New Creation can grasp while limited by a human mind. But 'when he appears, we shall be like him, for we shall see him as he is' (1 Jn 3:2).

Because of stunted growth for one reason or another, this appearing could be quite a culture shock for some! Growth comes from activity, and the activity of the New Creation must be examined more closely soon.

Meanwhile, one other fundamental characteristic of the New Creation is weakness. When I first became a Christian, in the spiritual sense as opposed to the cultural sense, I looked forward to the time when I would develop huge spiritual biceps and be able to fight for God, overcoming the devil and all his angels in the strength God would give me! As some would expect, it hasn't worked out like that at all. Within months, I learned from experience that there were ethical victories which I experienced before becoming a Christian which now were defeats. I could not explain this, and only by mental gymnastics was I able to continue. Since those days, God has continually pulled the rug from under my feet and from the human point of view shown up inadequacies which have been at times embarrassingly public. Others also have read the words of Paul, 'I can do all things through Christ' without giving enough attention to the last two words (Gal 4:13). It was with some stirring of heart that I first understood the words of the Lord Jesus when he said 'Out from myself I can do nothing'—and he was speaking as perfect man. 'It is the Father in me, who does the work' (Jn 14:10). My defeats were caused by my seeking to live on the basis of the normal human points of reference instead of out of the Fifth Dimension which is invisible and seen only by revelation.

The New Creation is created by God, designedly weak, but indwelt by almighty God in the Lord Jesus. But now, how is it to accomplish the will of God which is the desire of every true child of God? The foundation of which Paul speaks is laid. How shall we build with the right materials? Indeed, in respect of the 'good works' for which we have been created in Christ Jesus, which works God has prepared in advance for us to do (Eph 2:10), how do we find out what we should be doing anyhow? Until we know the answer to that question, we can easily be putting up the wrong building, or equally mistakenly, be using the wrong materials!

6

Guidance for the New Creation

Many books have been written on the matter of guidance. Any Christian worth his salt wishes to know what God wants him or her to do. Eventually, he learns to his great relief and joy that God does not expect him to live the Christian life. There is only one person who can do that, and it is the Lord Jesus Christ who lives in him. Christian living is to be Christ expressing his life through the Christian. But in what way does Christ wish to be released through him? It is wonderful to let Philippians 2:13 soak into our thinking. 'It is God who works in you to will and to act according to His good purpose.' Here is Christ working out from the New Creation in which he lives, first of all willing his will, and then doing it! But left like that, it is all ivory tower stuff. He must will his will through MY will; he must act through MY body. My theology must wear boots—it must 'touch the ground where I am standing.'

Hence all those books on guidance. We can find

all kinds of recommendations. Circumstances; logic; advice of mature Christians, individuals or as a company of people; much study of the Bible; the examination of various needs in the world, near or far, and so on. And of course prayer, which can lead to the witness of the Spirit . . . whatever that is and however differentiated from my own hopes.

I admit that all sounds rather ironic and even patronising. I am sorry about that. The fact is that I have in the past followed along all that trail and I have seen others do it also, and then often the future has demonstrated that we have finished up with religious activity, well motivated, but rather painfully recognised as at best a mistake, and almost certainly 'wood, hay and stubble'. Humble repentance before God has alone cleaned up the situation and opened the way for a new start, often to the mystification of friends. There has not been the creative flow of the Spirit; there has been very little evidence of the abundant fruit-bearing that our Lord spoke of as recorded in the Gospel of John, chapter 15 . . . a branch pruned so that it bears much fruit, however that fruit may be interpreted. No wonder that the apostle Paul exhorts the Corinthians to examine themselves to see whether they are still in the faith. 'Do you not realise that Christ Jesus is in you?' (2 Cor 13:5). All the suggested human activities are good, but not as a final basis for action.

Probably our main problem is that we are activity orientated, when the New Creation should be rest orientated. The Lord Jesus did not invite us (command us?) to come to him and labour (Mt 11:28–30). It was that we should come to him to rest! I know that this can and should be applied to the situation when we need his salvation. We must stop our own efforts to deserve this, and rest in his accomplished work when he died and rose again. But he speaks of taking a yoke, the yoke he is bearing; that is, joining him in the work he is doing. He tells us how this is done—by finding rest for our souls in service—rest from our own efforts to serve him. This can only mean joining him in the realm of the Spirit—the Fifth Dimension. We give up all our ideas of how we would serve him; we leave at one side all our likes and dislikes; we give up (not merely give) to him all our talents and qualifications—he may not want to use them as we think; what we are and what we have are placed in his hands, and whether he chooses to use us and them or not is up to him. It is not merely a matter of 'I surrender all' but 'I abandon all'.

We cannot use our talents for God and build in 'gold, silver and precious stones'.

There is a philosophy around which suggests that when we do not know what to do, we should start doing something, and then God will guide. 'You cannot guide a stationary boat' (even God cannot!) goes the argument. Well, maybe. But you may find unnecessary storms, much loss, and quite a bit of back-travelling (repentance) to do simply because you were not acting in faith. 'If you do not know what to do, then do something in faith' is as human as human can be. It is presumption, maybe.

But it is not faith. Faith is born in rest, by revelation, if we are talking of spiritual things.

The writer of the Letter to the Hebrews is much concerned with this aspect of spiritual life. In his continuing argument through chapter three into chapter four it seems that he is initially concerned about our acceptance of salvation by grace through faith alone. 'Now we who have believed (the Good News) enter into that rest, just as God has said, 'So I declared on oath in my anger, "They (the disobedient) shall never enter my rest"'' (Heb 4:3). But later, in verses 9 to 12 it is clear that he passes on to general principle, an ongoing from the question of salvation to that of general spiritual life. 'There remains then a Sabbath rest for the people of God, for anyone who enters God's rest also rests from his own work, just as God did from his' (Gen 2:2,3). 'Let us, therefore, make every effort to enter that rest, so that no-one falls . . .' (Heb 4:10).

From the time of our realised need of salvation and onwards, true faith is response to what God reveals. He shows us our need; he shows us that the Lord Jesus meets that need; we respond and find salvation—by faith. Not a leap in the dark, but a step into the light, leaving behind our old selves and self effort. Life hereafter cannot be the same.

If you have ever taken part in life-saving someone who is drowning, you will know that the hardest thing is to stop the person from struggling. One is very much activity orientated in those circumstances! If only such a person would 'rest' on his back, he would probably float. In any case, even extreme measures must be taken to make the drowning person 'rest' or risk the death of both parties. Activity orientation—death. Rest orientation—life.

But we must look more closely at the matter of rest and revelation. We are at the entrance into the Fifth Dimension.

7

Operating from Rest

For a very short time I was privileged to work in India. Though short, it was a time when I learnt much about that lovely but needy country, about myself, and about the way in which the Holy Spirit can work. One of the high spots was a time of ministry at a Holy Convocation (Spiritual Convention). There were several thousands of people there, and eight hours was not an unusual length of meeting! I spoke by interpretation, of course. There was much to learn from the manner in which these gatherings were conducted, although naturally some of the ways of doing things would be impossible in the West. On the other hand, close fellowship with the leader gave the opportunity for questions and testimony.

Apparently, he came to know the Lord in Canada and returned in due course with a great burden for his people in India. Wherever he knew that the gospel had not been preached, there he dashed. Here someone, there someone else, turned to the

Lord. However all he could then do was to leave them in the midst of a hostile Hindu community.

But one day, God spoke to him and in effect said 'Sit down! Now you are not to do anything unless I show it to you.' He obeyed.

For six weeks he did nothing but sit and read his Bible. And people talked. They always will, when someone obeys God and he asks for something a little unusual. Then one day, God said to him, 'Go and preach in *that* village.'

When he did so, a small group of Christians came into being! 'Go and speak to *that* man', and that man would come to the Lord and be a key man to a whole market area. That leader became much in demand, but he learned to recognise the voice of God in the inner rest which he maintained after that original crisis.

Two or three things came to me vividly, and I have sought to put them into effect in the intervening thirty years or more. The first was that when the need to operate from rest becomes known, this can quite normally lead to a kind of crisis, sometimes even seen by others, when the first deep adjustment is made. Then there is the walk as we respond to what God says. More of that later. But in view of the fact that initially this could be adjustment of personal relationships, it can be a painful time until things are put right. Once that is done, however, peace and light and the thrill of a deep realised union with the Lord Jesus possesses us. External demonstrations are beside the point. Alongside the inner experience, they are superficial!

This initial crisis and adjustment can be rather devastating. We may well have to alter our time-table somewhat in order to make time available. My wife and I, with a family, used to arrange a day which we would split in terms of responsibility for the young children, and feeding them. (We would fast.) Finally, in the evening, we could be together. We would sense when this was necessary, because reality insists that I say that this 'rest' of which I write is a focal point of attack from the Enemy. Our 'own works' never worry him—they are fruitless in the end. But the rest out of which spiritual building takes place is another thing! A sudden realised stumble can be apologised for, and rest be regained. But there is also a subtle build up, which calls for more drastic action.

When I first came to know the Lord, it was the understood thing that one spent a time, length undefined, with the Lord in prayer and Bible reading every day.

An alarm clock was a part of one's spiritual equipment! Among other things it is here that the 'rest' can be established for the launch into the day once one has learned the need of this. It is here that the voice of the Lord is heard in the Spirit. Start early enough, and it is not a hurried time. But from observation I would say that this practice is not so widespread as it used to be. One result is that Christians are more concerned with structures than real life in the Spirit. Another is a greater concern with personal blessing than with the accomplishment of the purposes of God in the world.

It is from the position of rest that we become not only aware of what the Lord wishes to do creatively through us, but also that the resources available to us from the Fifth Dimension are far beyond what we consider our talents and abilities. Starting from knowing that we cannot of ourselves accomplish the will of God anyhow, we are able to set no limits on his working through us. It is important to note that this applies whether his will is to sweep the roads, preach a sermon, visit an old lady, bring into being a significant arm of the Church or anything else.

Without faith, it is impossible to please God (Heb 11:6) and that which does not come from faith is sin (Rom 14:23). But previously we have seen that faith is response to the revelation of God. That is why it can be called substance (Heb 11:1). If we face these scriptures without rationalisation and accept that we should live by faith (Hab 2:4, Gal 3:11) then it is a sobering thought that too much so-called Christian work is not pleasing to God, is sin, and is dead. Religious, but not spiritual.

8

Activity of the Living Christ

I am persuaded that one reason for the length of the
Bible is that it must be addressed to every aspect of
the Christian life. When expounding some truth
from it, however, only one or two threads of the
total tapestry can be followed. They are obviously
related to much else in the written word, and this
can be a temptation to go on and on and on. As far
as possible I want to keep to the thread which
outlines the truth concerning the Fifth Dimension
and the necessity of our working out from it.

Already, however, this has meant taking ser-
iously the whole matter of spiritual rest. And
within that aspect again the need of abandonment
as a logical step. That the nature of faith and its
necessity in Christian service arises should now be
indicating that we are not looking at a passive mental or physical condition when speaking of this
biblical rest. Although we have lost something (if
ever we possessed it generally) in the lack of meditation practiced among Christians, I am not

advocating an 'emptying of the mind' or any such thing as concentrating on some mantra or object. From the truly spiritual point of view this can be dangerous even though it does open us to some powers of the invisible.

The rest of the Christian, as well as his race, is controlled by his 'looking away to the Lord Jesus'. 'Fixing our eyes on the Lord Jesus' (Heb 12:2). It is very easy to remain conscious of the presence of a loved one and yet to relax. There is even communication without verbal expression. Human experiences cannot fully illustrate the possible relationship with our Lord, but they can give us a clue.

So our rest in the Lord Jesus, who is our Sabbath, is an expectant, living, even vibrant experience. But expectant of what? One thing we can expect is an outworking of his invitation to take up the cross in order to follow him. In this context, the cross is some element of suffering or loss which God allows (sends?) into our lives which we can embrace ('take up') or resist (avoid). While we can learn to handle any unavoidable trouble redemptively, a cross is a loss which we can choose to take up or avoid. The wonder of it all is that every cross taken up means life for others, and a fuller life for ourselves; as indeed it was for our Lord.

The same principle of death and resurrection applies to our talents and human resources. The natural is first, and then the spiritual by resurrection. (1 Cor 15:46 as applied to the spiritual principle.) When my wife and I moved into Mission service after learning much of the 'cross life' in our everyday home-life, we each had to allow many things to die. One thing in my own experience has been remarkably interesting. In prospect there seemed no use for any subject in which I was proficient and experienced in my professional degree. There was no question of, can God use my this, that and the other in this proposed move? On the face of it, the answer would be no, in any case. Fortunately, we knew a little about the matter experimentally, and therefore knew what God was about, but not how! Out of every death in the spirit, there is inevitably a resurrection but the body (the how) was at God's choosing. Looking back, I can see that absolutely no aspect of my degree has not 'risen' and been used in a spiritual manner for the advancement of the kingdom of God! But *I* did not use them or choose the manner. That spiritual resurrection came about by responding to revelation given to me in rest. This kind of thing can be the everyday experience of anyone, because God is faithful to his Word and seeks to give himself through us to a world in need. We are not 'the pole on which is displayed the Son of God' in spite of the undoubted spirituality of the man who wrote that. We are the people through whom the no longer crucified Christ is demonstrated and his life shared with the world.

I am the first to agree that it is more important to be than to do. But this must be taken in a progressively purposeful way. The boots that our theology wears are for going places. Put another way, our rest is an inner experience whereby we can receive revelation as to what we do. Every spiritual experience we have is intended to be a means whereby we can share the life of Christ with others more effectively. If it does not work out in this way, then we frustrate the grace of God (2 Cor 6:2). Activated in this way, we begin to do the good works which God has prepared in advance for us to do (Eph 2:10). And they could be anything, small or great, but with spiritual point, accomplished by the New Creation, and therefore 'gold, silver and precious stones' which will go through the fire. Now and for ever, like the New Creation itself, they belong to the Fifth Dimension which is inhabited by the I AM.

We should avoid the merely paranormal: the 'unknown guest' as some are beginning to call the experience. That there is for some people an inner prompting they find helpful in everyday life, especially business life, is undeniable. But the Christian does not find forces from the invisible a strange thing when he knows that the Enemy delights to imitate God if he can.

Moreover, the Scriptures warn us not to have dealings with such powers which is guarantee enough that they exist. Such powers will always deceive by pointing to success as the world understands it. The Holy Spirit is also pointing, but to a deeper experience with Christ in his sufferings for a world that needs to know of his redemption. That is the greatest success of all; that is the privilege that angels cannot share. We are married to Christ, and just as in the Christian marriage service it is 'for better or for worse' in material terms so it is with his bride. We develop the habit of inner rest, not caring how God works with us, and the Holy Spirit flows from our innermost being as naturally as breathing. 'Something' is accomplished, and we know it because it is the work he is doing. ('Take my yoke . . .')

We never work on the basis of 'What would Jesus do?' The answer to such a question is often purely speculative, because we often have no example or instruction on the issue at hand. But we do have the example of him who said, 'What I see the Father do, that I do' (Jn 5:19). And he lives in us to reveal to us what *he* is doing, if only we will be quiet enough to hear and see, 'looking away to the Lord Jesus' (Heb 12:2), and unafraid of all the implications of that. He is our life (Col 3:4).

9

'Learn of Me'

'Be still, and know that I am God' (Ps 46:10). True human stillness, which involves letting go everything we consider as being 'ours', is clearly the nearest we can get to ever-present-tense I AM. It is there that we can know him. This is something different from knowing about him, obviously. But much of our Christianity is knowing about God, as opposed to knowing him. We stand on what we believe, our creed or something of that nature. What we know can be something quite different in character. It is a good idea to check this out from time to time. Is the God I believe in actually the God I know? I can believe by academic study; I can only know by revelation and a response to it as far as God is concerned.

We can learn to maintain this rest in spirit—this 'peace of God'—in the midst of busy days, problems, opposition, and persecution if we accept the testimony of many of those who suffer for Christ's sake. One very practical thing is that although the body may get weary, there is rarely any inner tension. If that comes, it is a sign that we have moved away from God. 'Learn of me—find rest to your souls' (Mt 11:29). How I love that word 'learn'!

I have spent a lot of our time on this matter of the Sabbath rest in Christ. This is because it is the only base from which we can be spiritually involved in the work of God, and not be merely working for God.

And involved we must be. Anything else is sub-Christian. We are stunting the New Creation at birth. Babyhood is a natural stage of development. But spiritually speaking it is a grotesque anomaly to remain in babyhood throughout our Christian life. Creatively acting adults must be our objective. This comes about only by obeying God's will by faith as he reveals it to us when we rest. Anything else is mere religion. Positive rest—revelation—faith (which is demonstrated by action)—accomplishment: this is the sequence whether in terms of salvation or works. To know that the Lord Jesus is ministering through me in preaching, programming for radio, washing up, writing, nursing, caring for the children, gardening, driving—you name it—is a great blessing. And because he is doing it, it must be spiritually significant. We are building in gold, silver and precious stones. Our resources are in him. And seeing that he is raised to the heavenlies and we with him also—we are working out from the Fifth Dimension (Eph 2:6). The New Creation is at work.

10

The Home-Ground of the New Creation

Because God is I AM, he reveals himself and his ways in the Bible from his point of view. It is for this reason that, purely in human semantics, there seem to be contradictions from time to time. Clever men—puny by comparison with him who inhabits eternity—point this out merely because they insist in thinking of God in human terms. Their God is created in the image of man, which is the wrong way round, as we know. Sincere, but possibly foolish, men take their stand on one statement of revelation and ignore statements which appear to be opposite in meaning. Yet honest appraisal of Scripture has to admit that both are therein. So-called Armenianism and Calvinism are a case in point. Human thinking cannot reconcile them, and semantic gymnastics are unsatisfactory. But 'was saved' (destined), 'is saved' and 'can be saved' (human responsibility) are all one to the eternally present-tense one. We can expect his ways to be higher than ours, and his thoughts beyond our thinking, and therefore not understandable by us. But revelation assures us that both are true.

This fact must be realised if we are to accept our place in Christ and know in reality our access to resources in the Fifth Dimension. This must not be imagined as some sort of blessing of adequacy which God sends down on us! He says we are living in the midst of it. He says we are seated (at rest) in the heavenlies in and with Christ. (Eph 2 as previously mentioned). And yet only too clearly we are also living in this materialistic sin-ridden world. Accept the one, and we live in some mystic ivory tower. Accept the other, and we grub about forlornly and frustratedly in a world which only seems to breed death, even when it attempts to show the love of God. Take a leap of faith in response to revelation and accept both and the possibility of a dynamic life opens up which, channelled in the way God chooses, will share with others not merely the knowledge about Christ but also his actual life.

This 'revelation of the dichotomy' has a great bearing on the development of our theme. When writing his letter to the Ephesians, Paul begins by addressing people whom he states as being at Ephesus and in Christ. This might not strike us as being particularly strange until we read on. He speaks of the incomparable power that is working for us who believe, and goes on to speak of Christ who is seated (resting, work accomplished) at the right hand of the Father in the heavenly realms far above all rule and authority, power and dominion

. . . and with all things under his feet . . . head over everything for the Church which is his body . . . the fulness of him who fills everything in every way. Paul goes on to say that God raised us up with Christ (past tense) and seated us (note that word again) with him in the heavenly realm in Christ Jesus. (Eph 1:10–2:6). This is an expansion of Paul's opening words: 'you are in Ephesus, but you are also with Christ above all power in heavenly realms out of which you are to do that work which God prepared for us in advance.'

Am I on earth to try to do the will of God hopefully with his help, or am I already in heaven whence I can observe the purpose of God being fulfilled and be involved? The thoughts and ways which are outside the range of our thinking reveal that both are true. It is not straining Scripture to point out that John declares that no one has ever seen God except the one and only, who is at the Father's side, he has made him known (Jn 1:18). And the context shows that he is referring to Jesus Christ who was there with him. And yet, 'is at the Father's side.'

It is a fact of the New Creation that its 'home ground' is in the invisible heavenlies in Christ. But at the same time, in and through us it lives on this earth. In mere words this has a theological interest. But in revelation, it has a dynamic which transforms the quality and service of the Christian. That revelation comes when we seek it in positive rest, looking away to Jesus as we meditate on the seemingly opposing truths.

The possible reason why many miss this dramatic introduction into the Fifth Dimension is the fundamental demand for the abandonment of ourselves to God to obtain his rest. We also sense that once we have made the discovery, it will call for action which almost certainly will be sacrificial in the end. Only a 'vision of Calvary' can motivate us here.

This is right. Action becomes faith at work. But that faith will express the very outgoing and redemptive life of Christ no matter what form it takes on. But it will inevitably be in character with the Lord himself, because he can only live his own life out from the invisible Fifth Dimension through us. We begin to live his life—which is just another of those 'contradictions'.

I I

The Inner Revelation of Christ

'Divine service held here three times a day'—a
notice over the sink in a kitchen! You have probably seen it somewhere yourself. I first saw it at a
Bible College and thought it was a healthy
reminder in the light of what I had been sharing
with the students an hour or so previously.

One rather thoughtless comment which may be
made concerning the things we have been considering is that we are so caught up in the every day
matters that we haven't time to set aside hours for
meditation. And it is true that I have implied that
meditation may be largely a lost art in our modern
western-style world. Yet, at the same time, I have
called for meditation in order to be spiritually
effective (as opposed to merely religiously demon-
strative). Two things are obvious: one is that we
have all the time that is necessary to do God's will;
the other is that my references to meditation do not
suggest that we go about our day in a sort of
spiritual daze, or shut away in our holy sanctum.

59

At certain times it may well be that we are constrained by the Holy Spirit to 'come aside' for a period. The 'prayer days' I have referred to in our family are an example. History suggests that this has been at the time of some sort of crisis, or a time when it was necessary to come to a decision on some issue which was not clear yet. But generally we have to set about the washing up, or changing the baby's nappies (diapers) or something equally time consuming and very much of 'this world'. Then what?

So much will depend on good habits developed. Is that time at the beginning of the day something which is normally spent quietly with God? If it is missed, is it an occasion which is forced upon us by circumstances and which we can confidently commit to our Father? If so, a person who has been totally obedient in love (no 'must' about it; no legalistic observance of even our times with God alone) will have eventually touched the experience spoken of by Paul in his letter to the Galatians (1:15–16) namely: 'revealed his son in me'.

Notice that we have passed through the theological truth into the realm of revelation and the experience on which the theology is formed. Why be satisfied with the 'belief' when the 'fact' can be ours? Some translations will say 'revealed to me', and of course that can be true, but it falls short of the actual statement of what was Paul's experience and what can be ours (2 Cor 13:5 inter alia).

It was Tozer, the writer of many books about the deeper things of God, who described this experience in very relevant everyday terms. He speaks of being in an unlit room on a dark night with the curtains drawn. Awake, one becomes conscious of someone being in the room, but unseen. It may be a friend or a burglar, either of which calls for appropriate action by us. The point is that it is not a rare experience to be aware of personality without seeing the person. There is nothing 'spooky' about it; nearly all of us can remember such experiences. Well, says Tozer, (and I confirm that he is right), one becomes aware of the Lord Jesus within (revealed in me) without seeing him as a person. We are conscious of his presence, but he is invisible. This should not be thought too strange. If Christ dwells in us as the Scripture says, is it unlikely that he who is almighty God, the I AM, should make his presence known?

Like any aspect of true living, we can always seek a deeper experience of it. But even a glimmer of this truth will set the heart free and enable the washing up, changing the nappies or any other 'secular' occupation become Christ working through me, and therefore 'divine service'.

It is here, perhaps, that the most common excuse for inaction in the service of God is presented. An excuse from involvement with God himself in prayer, sacrifice, and activity. And it sounds so humble! 'I'm afraid I must confess that my faith is very small. I could not become creatively, redemptively involved. I am of the earth earthy.' We begin to realise that this is only an excuse when we read that the treasure of the indwelling Christ is indeed in clay pots, earthen vessels (2 Cor 4:7). We are not being 'humble', we are stating facts! Let us then look at an example in the lives of the disciples, and a tremendous declaration in the writings of Paul.

The incident of the fig tree which was cursed by the Lord Jesus, and which died quickly, was the occasion for the disciples to raise the matter of faith. In Mark 11:22, the writer goes to the heart of the matter in quoting the Lord Jesus as saying: 'Have faith in God.' We are inclined to have faith only in our faith! But the strength of faith is in its object, not in the one who exercises it. We must expect God to work, not our faith.

And yet there is a quality of faith which does attach itself to God as a matter of course. This truth stems right back to the fact that we are a New Creation. The old person, with its big, little or no faith, is dead. We have been released, because God has made us alive as a New Creation. And this New Creation has a faith which, like itself, belongs to the Fifth Dimension which is the 'heavenlies' in Christ. Paul declares this in his own inimitable way and with incomparable logic and simplicity. If we will but begin to live out logically the life of the New Creation which is now us, the mystic truth of the deep things of God become clear even if inexplicable in human words alone. For, writes Paul, I (we) am crucified with Christ. This is the fundamental necessity of Christian experience. Then he states the obvious: nevertheless, I live. Of course; God has his purposes to work out through the New Creation and the body and personality in which it lives. But, says Paul, don't get me wrong. It isn't really me who lives (how could it be, if I am crucified with Christ?) but Christ who lives in me. It's all there in Galatians 2:20.

But he is still called to live by faith as we all are. That is to say, this New Creation which exists by Christ living in the new me must live by faith. However, by whose faith, if I am dead? The one logical answer, which I only reject by unbelief if I do so, is that it is the faith of Christ! So Paul boldly declares—'And the life I now live I live by the faith of the Son of God.' An alternative translation which says 'faith in' is true, but entirely illogical in the context of Paul's exposition.

'The faith of Christ'—I may only possess this to the size of a mustard seed as yet, but now I understand why it could remove mountains in the will of God! Attached to him, I can draw on every needed resource from the Fifth Dimension to accomplish his will revealed to me when I am in rest. Material, physical, financial, spiritual, wisdom—that faith will grow.

Rest, conscious union with him, a deepening knowledge of the unseen Christ within at work, a fullness of life in the Spirit accomplishing his will— all this and much more becomes our privilege by the grace of God.

How nearly—how nearly—I missed it!

12

The Fight from Rest

It may seem illogical to write so much about 'rest' and then to start writing about 'fighting'! But no one can pretend that this issue can be avoided. Our Lord obviously had times of battle, and not least in the Garden of Gethsemane prior to his arrest, so-called trial, and eventual execution on a cross. It is not without significance to our theme that after his experience in the Garden, he goes steadily through to the bleakest experience of all.

But Paul writes to Timothy to 'fight the good fight holding on to faith' (1 Tim 1:18–19) and later (6:12) exhorts him 'Fight the good fight of the faith.' Finally, of himself he writes 'I have fought the good fight . . . I have kept the faith.' (2 Tim 4:7).

What is this 'faith' that all the fighting has been about? Certainly not doctrine. Certainly not some form of Church government or practice. And what aspect then of the Christian experience is under attack? Because it is fundamental, essential to all true spirituality, I believe and know from experience that it is the true rest which the writer to the Hebrews exhorts us to obtain (Heb 4). The enemy tries through various forms of circumstances to tempt us to abandon our rest. If he succeeds, nothing we do will really trouble him. It is the activity of the New Creation responding in faith to the revelation of the will of God which confounds him all the time. And that activity begins and is rooted in 'rest'. Like the fox in the nursery story of the Little Pigs, he can huff and puff and blow down anything of wood, hay and stubble! He doesn't mind if a religious appearance remains, so long as he has been able to destroy the spiritual potential of something he cannot touch.

If he can provoke us to activity, he has won. You will have noticed that all the references mentioned above where Paul speaks of fighting, he relates it to faith. It is true that we may eventually do something sooner or later, but that will be in response to something that God shows us. It will be God at work in and through us as we rest. No tension. No spiritual exhaustion. We fight to take our stand in what God has done and given us, and move out from there as and when and in whatever manner he shows. We have fought the fight of faith.

We can even be tempted to seek to pattern our life and service on that of some great man of God. Having started in faith we have slipped into 'works'—activity without God in it. If we rest in abandonment to him, he will show us what he wants to work out through us as a result of that other life fulfilling the purpose of God for it. The story has been truly used by the Holy Spirit.

But what about Ephesians chapter six? Verse 10 onwards. This is Paul's wonderful illustration of Christian warfare based on the Roman soldier to whom he was probably chained. He illustrates the Christian's position in Christ by the armour his guard is wearing. Among other things, he notices by implication that the soldier has no defence behind him! He has a shield and sword. These last two are very important to him—and as object lessons, they are very important to us.

Study the text of Ephesians 6:10 onwards. What does Paul tell us to do in our armour—which is the completed work of Christ for us? He does not tell us to fight! He tells us to stand. 'Having done all', he says 'Stand!' with your armour well in place.

We know that in verse 12 he speaks of our 'struggle', our 'wrestling', with rulers, authorities . . . spiritual powers of evil in heavenly places. But it is very important to know that the Greek word used for wrestling, struggling, and so on means hand to hand fighting. The 'wrestling' of the King James version is well chosen. How well that fits Paul's exhortation to us to stand well covered by our armour! He knew even better than we do that one does not wrestle in armour with a sword in one hand and a shield in another!

In the Fifth Dimension we are far above all powers known and unknown. We have seen that from the second chapter of Ephesians. We fight by taking our stand in that realm where we rest. Using our shield of faith against all the insinuating fiery darts of the devil, and resting in the revelation given through the Scriptures, the Sword of the Spirit, we stand and do not resort to the wisdom, tactics and powers of this world. To do so, would be to come down from our high position in Christ (our armour) and therefore we experimentally step out of him. Then indeed we are in hand to hand fighting with those powers, and we don't stand a chance. 'Stand therefore!' says Paul. Refuse condemnation; refuse worldly tactics; 'Stand'—it is a picture word for an alert 'rest'. We have been raised with the Lord Jesus far above all principalities. We must not agree with the devil when he contradicts God, as is his habit from the beginning of time. 'Has God said . . .?'

I will share another of my simple stories. It is a true one; the little girl concerned is now quite grown up and will not recognise herself. She had just been tucked up in bed for the night. As Mother went to leave her, she said: 'Mummie, Satan came and knocked at my heart's door today.' How spiritually expressed, Mother thought, just to get a few more moments before the light went out! But she played along: 'So what did you do?' she queried. The answer made her realise that this was not just to spin out time. 'I asked Jesus to answer the door', the little one replied. Gently, Mother asked 'And what happened then?' Came the bright and anything but sleepy reply: 'Satan said, "Sorry! I thought someone else lived here." and he went away'!

'Out of the mouths of babes and sucklings Thou hast ordained praise.'

13

Acceptable Failures

A very dear friend of mine, who has been in his time something of a public figure, was once asked, 'Do you believe in sinless perfection?' Like a number of people, he had faced this one before! With a gentle smile he replied: 'Well, it's not a bad thing to aim at, is it.' Both sin and perfection call for definition if the question is asked in reference to Christian experience as opposed to mere theology.

As with many other areas, it is not failure to realise that activities for God have been largely a matter of human religiosity. This can be confessed, and cleansing received. Similarly, every new revelation of spiritual truth and life calls for a new start in that sphere. Initial elements of failure are not blameworthy. But too low an aim is criminal. To know that there is a higher way and not to seek to take it is to sin.

There is something loveable and charming about the efforts of a child to get around after it leaves the confines of the cradle. But after a while, much to the delight of its parents, it seems to tire of crawling and generally pushing around on its bottom. It can see that there is a better way of doing things—its parents move around perpendicularly. By pulling itself up against a chair-leg or mother's knee or something, it launches into its first staggering steps. We know the result. It bumps down on its nappies. Parents coo and laugh, and encourage further efforts. If things go normally, the time comes when the child walks, runs, jumps without even thinking about it. The child is not blamed for the initial failures. However if the child does not develop in this way, but remains trapped in its babyhood, we are faced with a tragedy. The normal becomes sub-normal.

I hope the simplicity of the illustration will not tempt anyone to ignore its application. Just because much of past activity has been wrongly orientated, or because not much success has crowned efforts to walk in the Spirit, these are no reasons to accept the suggestion that 'This is not for me' or the lie that 'This that I thought was revelation is only a mirage'. Both suggestions are obviously from the devil because they are discouragement. Father says 'You are weak, and will always be so. But I am your Life and Strength. Get up, and by my grace, press on. Such life will always amaze you, but it will become more and more the normal.'

We may 'bump our nappies' a thousand times, but the thousand-and-first time will see us going on to run.

God does not expect a 100% appropriation of his

truth into experience all at once. When he tells us to come to him for rest, he says 'learn of me'. Paul states significantly that he has learned in whatever state he finds himself to rest (be content). What is rightly demanded is that we see something of the light ahead, and go toward it. 'Forgetting the things behind' says Paul, 'I press towards the mark' (Phil 3:13,14). He sees in the Spirit what he is aiming at. Having truly found the rest which is for the people of God (Heb 4:9) we shall learn to walk only by faith, which is responding to what God shows.

One of the hardest parts of expectant rest is the time during which we give glory to God by believing, just as Abraham did (Rom 4:20–21). And wait. It has been said that patience is 75% of faith! Certainly, in response to pressure from people who do not understand, or one's own activity-orientated outlook, it is a great temptation to 'get moving'. Our fellowship with the indwelling Christ will keep us steady. And he may well have to sort out some of our motivations by showing us that our aim is lower than his will.

14

Much Closer Than a Brother

Another name for the life from the Fifth Dimension could well be the Resurrection Life. Because God has united us to Christ in redemption, he states precisely that we are raised with him to sit (rest) in the heavenlies. This we looked at previously in relation to Ephesians chapter two. One way of describing the situation would be to say that resurrection life is the quality of life that we live out from the Fifth Dimension, which has within it all the resources for the accomplishment of God's will. No other dimension or series of dimensions contains this. The two go together, and neither is more than a theological concept unless they do link up in experience.

We have already seen that by definition there must be a death before there is a resurrection. This is where the value of the 'natural' comes in. We do not despise it or reject it. We use it, whether it is in terms of our talents or our possessions. Without the natural, which can die, there can be no resurrection. Once the 'music of the cross' is heard, we are able to cry with Paul that all we are in status or background, all the acquired knowledge we may have accumulated, all the possessions which have come to hand, are but rubbish and food for the resurrection and knowledge of Christ (Phil 3:8–10).

From this point, no matter how we are occupied in the daily round, we know that it is Christ from within who is working through us. The burdens, the problems, the pains of life, are but his dying through us on the cross we have taken up. Paul boldly declares that we go about bearing in our bodies the dying of the Lord Jesus (2 Cor 4:7–10). The privilege of this has to be realised in worship. This is not the dying of our old lives: that was accomplished on the cross in Christ.

In ways we scarcely realise, we often live as if in Old Testament times. This is not to deny that God speaks through the Old Testament scriptures. Particularly is this true of the Psalmists, the Prophets and the lives of the Old Testament 'saints'. But when we echo their understanding of God, we are quite often less than we need be. We may quote, for instance, that there is one who stays closer than a brother (Prov 19:24). We have in mind the Lord Jesus. In a sense this is true, but there is an overriding truth which is greater. Paul says that this truth had been hidden right up to his time, but was then revealed (Eph 3:2–11). This 'mystery' had been hidden for ages, but then God made known the glorious riches of this mystery which is Christ in you. Not just the laws of God written in the heart, as Isaiah and Jeremiah had seen it, but indwelt by him who is the very fulfilment of the Law.

We have to learn to live not by one who is just 'there', but by one who is 'right in here'! But because God is the I AM and omnipresent, he is indeed everywhere, but unseen. Thus the Fifth Dimension is not somewhere 'up there', but in us and around us. 'The Kingdom of God is within (among) you' (Lk 17:21).

In him, we live and move and have our being (Acts 12:28). How impoverished and stunted most of our lives are by comparison with what God has in mind! Directly related to and dependent on the Lord Jesus Christ, we can work out from rest by faith in response to his revelation of what he wishes to do through us and in the process of that, we can enjoy to a small degree what eternal life is like.

I wrote 'can work out from rest'. In fact, we must do this if we are to be involved in building his church worldwide, beginning at our 'Jerusalem' and reaching out to the uttermost parts. And, perhaps more importantly from our individual point of view, if we are going to do 'works that will go safely through the fire'. Which fire? Hell fire? Where is hell, if God is everywhere?

We have gone along a main line of a thread in the intricate pattern of spiritual life which only issues from rest, and noticed one or two cross threads on the way. Eventually, we must look at the unavoidable issue which faces us all: the hereafter.

15

God, A Consuming Fire . . .

At this point, we have to consider some of the most simple and most difficult things about God. Some we can understand within our human reasoning. Others, though simply expressed in words, are nevertheless difficult if not impossible to grasp. However, in all of them there are logical consequences also which in themselves may be difficult to accept. But this will be largely on account of preconceived ideas or built-in prejudices.

He is the I AM, the eternal present-tense God. We have looked at that, and considered some of its implications. Immediately we were faced with the fact that his thinking and ways can be far and away above ours. Revelation can reveal some of this to the heart, but even then it may not be possible or permitted to express it in human words sometimes. 'We speak in words taught us by the Spirit' (1 Cor 2:13). 'Groans that words cannot express' (Rom 8:26). 'Heard inexpressible things that man is not permitted to tell' (2 Cor 12:4). It is only the New

Creation which can have this union and communion with the I AM. It happens in the Fifth Dimension, but has its impact in this four dimensional world.

God is love. But that very fact means that he can hate. This he has expressed towards sin and all kinds of formality which prevents direct union with him. He is light. But he is also a consuming fire. A consuming fire. Fire destroys things it burns; its cleansing power lies in what is left when it destroys. It does not cleanse that which it destroys. In redemption, God expresses himself as light. 'I am the light of the world' declared the Lord Jesus (Jn 8:12). But in judgement, he expresses himself as fire. He speaks of sending his angels in the last time and 'they will weed out of his kingdom everything that causes evil and all who do evil. They will throw them into the fiery furnace (Mt 13:42). And also, 'It is better to enter into life maimed than with two hands to go into hell where the fire never goes out' (Mk 9:43). In both the positive and the negative there is a measure of picture language, but the consistent references to fire in connection with a 'lost eternity'—we have noted but two—cannot be avoided.

The I AM who inhabits eternity, is omnipresent. We accept that rather glibly, noting that David, the psalmist, declared that 'Whether in heaven or hell, east or west, night or day, God is there' (Ps 139:8–12). But if this Great Positive (Light) and Great Negative (Fire) is everywhere without exception, then we can only conclude that heaven and hell are in him. That may not make sense at first, because we think in human terms and rather subjectively. Preconceptions, prejudices, keep us reasoning from the normal points of reference; four dimensional thinking. But the New Creation can, and must, accept truth which is only seen in reference to the Fifth Dimension by revelation, 'far above—and high as the heavens are above the earth' which comes out from the spiritual reality of the invisible.

The writer C S Lewis brought to bear on many spiritual matters an incisive mind which could express itself in allegory, parable, theology, humour and deep simple truth. In his book *Screwtape Letters* he purports to have collected a number of letters written by The Father Below to a Junior Tempter living above him on earth. They all concern a Christian who is attended by the Junior Tempter, whose job it is to make the new Christian as ineffective as possible. Towards the end of the series, it would seem that the Christian is killed by a bomb. The Junior Tempter exults, until Screwtape really takes him to pieces for his stupidity in allowing the Christian to be killed. Now, he fumes, we can no longer touch him—and so on.

But there is a wonderful passage which is Screwtape's comment on the Christian's entry into the presence of his Lord. 'That searing fire' Screwtape's letter screams, 'That searing fire before which you cringed was to him cool light.' Our God is a consuming fire. To the spiritually dead, a searing flame—hell. To the New Creation, cool light—heaven. But it is the same God, who contains all and inhabits all.

The New Creation is 'at home' in the Fifth Dimension, and indwelt by God, has lived out from that invisible realm. There is no culture shock, any more than there was for Enoch, who 'walked with God, and was not' (Gen 5:24).

When I found some of these matters difficult to accept, I was reminded that our Lord said on one occasion that he could not tell his disciples all there was to know. 'I have much more to tell you, more than you can bear. But when he, the Spirit of truth comes, he will guide you into all truth.' (Jn 16:13). Here is obvious reference to the time after Pentecost. From the Old Testament we learn of God in history and in the lives of individuals. There we see his acts, and get to know his ways. It is the latter that are most important, because if 'They have not known my ways . . . they shall never enter my rest.' (Heb 3:10–11). But later, through the writings of Paul and others, we may pass on from the ways of God to the person of God. Let us enter that rest that we may know him.

16

. . . Or God as Cool Light

In the light of what we have seen from the Scriptures, the 'hereafter' is an entering into the realm of the eternal 'Now'. Hopefully, we have been living in the realisation of its reality, and living out from its resources. But of course, this is not an unfettered release into a vast nothingness; it is rather an ultimate conscious seeing him who is the I AM without anything to cloud our sight or lessen our feeling of him. Above all it is a point of no return.

Then, for as long as the eternal present tense exists, we are what we are. The New Creation, born of the Spirit of God himself, is perfectly at home and spends that time in service, praise, worship. God, perfect in love, who indeed is love, is said to rejoice in that completely realised union with himself as much as those who are called his children. Human words have always failed to express adequately the exquisite nature of that time, as the inspired but mysterious language of the Revelation at the end of the Bible testifies.

But that 'cool light' in which the New Creation lives is also a consuming fire—a fire which destroys everything that can be destroyed and remains fire continually to that which cannot be consumed but which is spiritual in nature but not re-created. All that has issued from unrestored humanity, being wood, hay and stubble (to quote Paul) is dealt with. It is true that 'their works follow them', but it seems clear that only that which is 'gold, silver and precious stones' gets through the fire. All merely religious activity and works are finished. That which has been created through faith by the Holy Spirit operating through the New Creation remains to the glory of God. Once again, I would emphasise, this is not a question of motivation; the issue is the character—one could say the quality—of the works themselves which are motivated by revelation if they are 'gold'. We have already studied how the truly spiritual work comes into being from rest, through revelation which is responded to by faith and worked out in the love and life of Christ, which is sacrificial as need be.

The teaching of Paul is clear enough as to the position of a Christian who does not work from rest—he will be saved but 'only as one escaping through the flames' (1 Cor 3:15). But what of the ordinary human being, judged by the light he has received and 'found wanting'? By the very nature of his being he finds himself experiencing God as fire!

Our Lord told the story of the rich man and

Lazarus (Lk 16:19–31). No matter what interpretation one puts on it, it makes terrible reading. Its detail confirms much else spoken of in the Bible regarding life after death. The point for us at the moment is that both the rich man and Lazarus were conscious of Abraham. The rich man—no longer rich in any sense—could communicate with Abraham, and recognise Lazarus. But all to no avail, either for himself or his family still living. The 'great chasm' that was fixed between the light and the fire is clearly one of experience and not of geography. It is the chasm between the spiritually living and the spiritually dead. A human is a spiritual being, and not just a living body. The loss of limbs does not lessen the being who lives in the body, even if it does hinder the activities of it. This partly explains the courage and will-power which so often enables the stricken person to live a meaningful life. And that spiritual being is eternal— either as a spiritually dead being or a spiritually alive one—a New Creation.

The fact of what we call hell does not cease to exist because we ignore it or do not believe in it, any more than that of heaven. It is a part of the eternal present to which we all travel.

17

The Enemy of Rest

In the early days of creation, it would seem that a supremely beautiful created angel aspired to be equal with its creator—the I AM. As a result of this contradiction of his own being, he was thrown onto this earth. The Lord Jesus said: 'I saw Satan fall like lightning from heaven' (Lk 10:18). He is also called 'The god of this age' by Paul (2 Cor 4:4). Indeed, when he had the opportunity of a direct confrontation with Christ, he claimed to rule the whole world, in that he offered its kingdoms to Christ if only he would bow down to him. It is noticeable that he who was the one through whom it had all been created did not deny the claim at that point (Lk 4:5). It was a subtle temptation to short-cut the way to the throne of this earth, excluding the need of redemption through his blood being shed on the Cross.

There is a line of thought which suggests that in view of the fact that from the beginning of creation, Satan has challenged the I AM regarding his right to rule, God, even God, would not take advantage of him by exercising his obviously available power to destroy him right away. Let not the cosmic creation be in the position of saying that the I AM who is Love is also despotic. The earlier revelation of him is now completed in the Lord Jesus, and in redemption on the Cross in utter weakness he has beaten Satan on his own ground. All Satan can now do in various forms is to repeat his unoriginal temptation 'Has God said . . .?' Some people fall for this because they have allowed their minds to be blinded. Even Christians can be deceived by his 'Has God said . . . that all your sin is forgiven; that he indwells you; that his grace and redemption are available to you when you allow sin to come in at times; that he is not afar off when you are in trouble and suffering; that those "other people" are not less than they should be, and that none can thwart you in your work? Has God said this, and more besides?'

As Christians, we can look forward to the time when Satan is finally taken from the scene. When Christ returns, we shall see 'the King in all His beauty' no matter how we may have seen him beforehand. But until that time, we need to remind ourselves of how our great deliverance was obtained. 'Do this in remembrance of me' (Lk 22:19) was his instruction linked with the 'visual aid' of the broken bread and the wine. It was to be a means of remembering, not a continual sacrifice. That has been made once and for all (Heb 9:25– 28).

In all our enjoyment of the wonder of our union with him in his ascended being, throughout all the thrill and privilege of seeing him work wonders through us in the fulfilment of his will to express his victory, we must not forget his agony of Gethsemane nor his spiritual death ('Why didst Thou forsake Me?') which delivered us from the grip of Satan through death. Being a spiritual death as well as a physical one means that we can enter into it and through it to resurrection as a New Creation. We must never forget the cost of all that which was inflicted on the I AM who is love.

The reality of our gratitude and worship for our Lord's suffering on our behalf will be easily measured by our response when he asks something from us or of us that costs. If we hold back anything or anybody, then we have never 'seen' Calvary. And the Holy Spirit will not have the freedom to reveal the living Christ within us. It will be our loss; but he will grieve.

He who has given everything can ask for anything—but wonderfully enough, that is true both ways in our relationship with him who is in union with us (Jn 14:13; Jn 16:24).

18

Priorities of the Fifth Dimension

Priorities in what one might call our social life are from time to time a matter of some discussion, especially among missionaries. Which comes first in my thinking, consideration, provision? Obviously God comes into the picture, and then there is the family (wife and children—and maybe even further out), and finally there is the 'work of God' which has been taken on.

The arguments rage back and forth. The family must come first before the work. No! The work of God must come first. The family must take second place. There are good arguments both ways. But you will have noticed already who has been left out of the argument. God.

When we have started out, or gone back to, complete abandonment to God and begun to live out from the Fifth Dimension, we see things in a different light. It is not that the same issues don't arise, and it is not that our responsibilities in some way change. It has to be said that sometimes decisions are made on the unrecognised basis of our own convenience and now that will change. While seeing all that is involved we are also conscious that there is a will within our will—the will of the one who indwells us and whom we have come to 'see' in the Spirit at least to some extent. If we will but receive it, we see things with his eyes. (Or perhaps he sees things with ours?) However it is, he reveals his thoughts on the situation and we can respond in faith, whether the solution to the question is as we would like it naturally speaking or not. Perhaps more difficult, his way may not be that which other people might expect us to take! That can be hard. Blessed is the one who has a wife or husband, or even a very close friend, who comes to the same conclusion because they know the dimension in which such ways are revealed. When God is really first, then, in the light of Calvary, nothing less than his will is good enough. And his will which is far above our understanding is something that is revealed, even when it seems to be 'normal'. This is something known in the private place of the Spirit. No other human, or company of humans, can make that decision, even if they are used to make some suggestion. Faith is response to what God reveals to the individual even if it is blessed with confirmation later by a fellowship of believers.

Of course, I am not speaking of an experience of a newly-born babe in Christ. Such a person will not normally have found the Fifth Dimension. Hopefully, he will have heard of it and will be seeking it. A young colt is trained just so far before it is put into harness with a yoke. Then it works with one other. 'Come, take my yoke upon you . . .' (Mt 11:29). It will always work then in line with the others who are bearing a similar yoke. But it will not be an extended yoke! 'What shall this man do?' 'What is that to you? You must follow me.' (Jn 21:21–22)

With all this at the heart of our living, we shall always be able to get our priorities right and if they are not in line with the current thinking of the community in which we live, we shall be given grace to press on with God.

'If you have the opportunity of being a missionary, don't worry about being a king!' So wrote or spoke someone. I appreciate the sentiment, having served as one for many years. (As a missionary, I mean!) But it is infinitely more important to be available as a channel for the life of God. For this to be true, one can sweep roads or run a business or throw in everything and go to the ends of the earth. But no one who has started to live out of the Fifth Dimension will ever work for his or her living again. They will see daily life as being the way God wants to share his life with others, and that therefore his promises to provide our need will be fulfilled. The declarations of our Lord recorded in Mt 6:24–34 are valid for all his children, not just for a few 'specials'. Particularly true is that of verse 33: 'Seek first his kingdom, and his righteousness, and all these things (food, clothing and so on) will be given to you as well.' How we seek and where we seek his kingdom are all wrapped up in the 'good works which God has prepared in advance for us to do' (Eph 2:10). And that is something which is revealed to us from the Fifth Dimension as we rest, and to which we respond in faith, eagerly, come what may. Not a few have gone overseas as missionaries who should never have gone; God did not send them. Equally there are many who should have gone, but who have refused the vision God wanted to give them. But there are those who have heard the call of Calvary, and who have from that time onwards seen the world and this life from his point of view, and are pressing on to a crown to lay at his feet and to hear his 'Well done!' And that can only be worked out in the place he puts us in—be it in suburbia or the jungles of Peru!

19

Believing—or Knowing?

I have already suggested that 'expectant rest' will almost certainly have a real element of waiting in connection with it. The grace to wait is probably a great gift from God. During it we give glory to God as did Abraham; in spite of seeming contradictions and 'skies of brass' we say in effect, 'Let every man (and devil) be a liar, but God is true.' It is a fantastic privilege to be trusted by God with something like this, and we are made bigger people in God in the process.

When we are born of the Holy Spirit we have within us all the potential for the full revelation of our union with Christ and the ability to live by his faith. The infant child has within it what the adult will be. There is nothing more that Christ has to do on our behalf. The work was accomplished in its entirety when he died and rose again. He indwells the New Creation by the Spirit from the beginning, just as the self-centred wilful self indwells the human baby from its beginning.

Theoretically, the Christian experience therefore should develop rather in the shape of a slope. There will be the bumps, more or less serious, of adolescence, but we should grow out of these and pass on to responsible adulthood. However, the facts of life are different in most cases. The 'upward journey' of development is more like a flight of stairs! Crisis after crisis. Some larger than others, but each taken at some cost. We even go down a stair sometimes—which can be even more painful than going up! Unfortunately, there are those of us who at some time decide we have had enough, and we settle at some convenient landing on the way. There are plenty of others there and as for those who pass on up, we think they are fanatics in some way.

Let us die climbing. All we have been considering up to this moment may already be our experience. If so, we shall only praise the Lord for his grace and patience. If not, then the new abandonment, the waiting for the new revelation of our union with Christ that will mean knowing (not just believing) that HE is our life, will be another crisis indeed. But it will be finally something that God does for us. As Paul the apostle puts it: 'When it pleased God to reveal his Son in me . . .' (Gal 1:16).

From that time onwards, we shall worship the living God, the great I AM, but we shall never try to work for him again. Our delight will be to be completely available to him so that he may work through us in whatever way he wishes. The peace of God will indeed possess us in a way which is beyond understanding. Our aim will be to enjoy our God but not ourselves. As Judson Cornwall saw faith, so shall we: 'The sin of presumption is forgivable, but since it so often masquerades as faith, it is seldom confessed as a sin' (*Unfeigned Faith*, Kingsway 1981, pp138–39). So often, therefore, it remains unforgiven! It is possible that we all need to repent to some degree. And then to rest and wait for his revelation.

We only know the fullness of the Holy Spirit as an ongoing experience to the degree we are conscious of his indwelling. The ministry of the Holy Spirit is not merely to bless us, but supremely to reveal the Lord Jesus. (Compare Acts 9:17 with Gal 1:16.)

20

A Different Kind of Person

It does not take us long to discover that we are living out from the invisible Fifth Dimension. Without any conscious effort on our part, we begin to find that we are a different person! Our attitudes towards people change; we do not mind the slights that come our way as confessed Christians; moreover, material things, while appreciated, cease to cause us any concern if we lack them or are constrained to give them away. We do not see suffering as some sort of punishment, or as having its source in some evil, even if that is also true. It becomes a means whereby in a spiritual way we share the sufferings of Christ. (2 Cor 1:5; 1 Pet 4:13.) Our faith is expressed more in giving than in getting, but we never lack any needed practical thing.

The reason for this—and much more—is simple. We are indeed a different person. We are a New Creation by which Christ is expressing himself. We are living out from the Fifth Dimension where Christ is reigning, and we reign with him.

The normal criteria of even good humanity are no longer final, and many of them do not apply at all.

The Lord Jesus once declared that out of the overflow of the heart, the mouth speaks (Mt 12:34). When a vessel is jogged, it is that of which it is full that spills out! We begin to find that some of the things we have previously said and sung seem to be a little foreign to us. We no longer sing 'Father, let me be yours and yours alone.' Rather do we prefer, 'Father, I will be yours and yours alone!' Anything that suggests separation from the Saviour sounds wrong in our ears. 'We come into your presence . . .' can be but a cliché at worst or the words of someone who does not know that the Lord is united with him in the everyday. We may recognise communally that fact with great blessing, but that is another thing and which is strengthened by a declaration of the precise fact—'We are in your presence together'. I would not wrangle over words; but they are powerful and will often reflect the heart condition.

Of course, we shall express ourselves in public prayer in a way that can be heard by all those who should hear us. But never shall we so raise our voice as to suggest that God is deaf and exists some miles away! What we say and how we say it will demonstrate the quality of our relationship in the Spirit. Somehow, our thinking will move over from ourselves, so that we say less of 'Bless me' or 'Use me (even me)' and more of 'Bless him, her or them' and 'Here am I, Lord, available for you to reach out to them by me, if you want to. Whether I am blessed, or even used in the process, is beside the point!'

'Be with us' becomes a silly request. Isn't he already there? 'Make us conscious of your presence' may certainly be valid if necessary, and not just to make us feel good. It could be a confession of coldness in fact. We no longer 'storm the heights of heaven' because we know that we are already there!

This is not just a matter of simple semantics. They express a heart condition which either has or has not recognised that we live out from the Fifth Dimension. Either they are the expressions of a sincere religious man or woman who has not yet given up on themselves in order to rest and to allow the Spirit to reveal who they are in the Lord Jesus; or, as the New Creation they express the longing to be set free and to live in the delight of the children of God; heirs of God, joint heirs with Christ (Rom 8:17). He longs to be about his Father's business, to co-operate by wearing the yoke that he is wearing.

We normally assert rightly that the work of the Lord Jesus is complete. Nothing can be added to it, and because it is sealed by his blood, nothing can be taken away. But he is not inactive. His present ministry is intercession (Rom 8:34). We can therefore recognise that the highest privilege we may know through our union with him is to have him interceding through us by the Holy Spirit (Rom 8:26). We do not have to strive in prayer. He gives himself through us. We should therefore be willing to forsake everything to allow this to happen—for the sake of the object of our intercession. It is a realm in which only the New Creation can live. It is the incense of the Fifth Dimension.

21

Resurrection Life—For Others

Each finger of the hand is different. Each can be studied to decide what contribution it makes, and how it makes it, to the action of the hand. In order to examine the New Creation and to understand to some extent the mystic miracle of its life and action, we have had to study briefly various other matters which are related to it. The fundamental fact is that it lives out from the invisible spiritual dimension which I have called the Fifth Dimension because the four dimensional world in which we live is only the sphere of its manifestation, and not its source of being. That is in the continuing 'now' of the God who is I AM, with whom we are in union through the redemptive work of Christ in all its fullness.

We do not have to understand this fully. Indeed, it is doubtful if we shall ever do that until we are still enough in physical death (or translation at his coming) to see him as he is. Although we can obviously become conscious of his presence, both in us and by us, we do not see him. To do so would be death (Ex 33:20) as we transfer from time to eternity.

When God needed to communicate with men and women through a visible being, he sent an angel—another being which was created, and therefore is a creature of time. When in fact he did wish to be seen for the work of redemption, he came as a man! That was all a part of his humbling of himself as we are told by Paul in the second chapter of his letter to the Philippians (verses 6–7). Although he is God, he came into this four dimensional world and existence in which sinful man, demons, and the devil himself live. No wonder he was often misunderstood! Like the New Creation he brought to birth, he did not belong here on earth. 'My kingdom is not of this world' (Jn 18:36). He was the I AM of the eternal now, and when he declared that, and it 'showed through' for a moment, his enemies cringed before him (Jn 18:5).

It is important that we should grasp as much of this aspect of God and his relationship with us as possible. This is the initial reason for our seeking to enter into the rest that God has provided (Heb 4:9). We can very easily become just believers. We believe it is true. It is a part of our theology. We can preach about it and uplift the Saviour. But that does not necessarily mean it is our possession.

Our theology should wear boots, as I have said. How often have we been exhorted from the platform or the printed page that we should persevere as did Paul, for example. 'I can do all things through Christ who is my strength' (Phil 4:13). 'I have been beaten, nearly drowned, thrown out and much else, and I count it all joy.' 'Persecuted, but not abandoned; perplexed but not in despair; struck down but not destroyed' (2 Cor 4:8,9). Great stuff! If Paul can do it for Christ, so can we—or at least, be ready for it, as I hope I am. That last part is often missing! The understandable reaction of many is well understood. That is all very well, but I am not a Paul. Some can even add that they have tried hardship and it hasn't worked! It should work, for there it is in Scripture for our example and encouragement. It is even more confounding when it is Jesus who did something and we cannot follow him.

The one thing we have not been told at the appropriate time is that Paul had a consciousness of the indwelling Christ. Jesus revealed IN him (Gal 1:15). The Lord Jesus, as perfect man, knew that the Father indwelt him (Jn 5:19).

It is that revelation, that possession as against merely believing it, that makes all the difference. Believing can be but the academic response to knowledge obtained. It is the beginning, but only that. Possession comes by revelation and the seeking of that revelation can be costly. It costs a lot of rubbish, says Paul! (Phil 3:8). But we have already seen the difference it makes in terms of the consciousness of the New Creation and the resources in the Fifth Dimension whereby our works are created by the Holy Spirit and are of the quality which can stand the fire of God as no other works can.

We become not only victorious. We become more than victors (Rom 8:37). We may suffer, but the indwelling one handles the situation, and we become bigger people in God. 'For our light and momentary troubles are achieving for us an eternal weight of glory that far outweighs them all. So we fix our eyes not on what is seen, but on what is unseen. For what is seen is temporary' (wood, hay, stubble at best), 'but what is unseen is eternal' (gold, silver and precious stones). (2 Cor 4:17–18). Every death leads inevitably to a resurrection—a fuller life.

And because it is the essence of his nature, ('always bearing about in our bodies the dying of the Lord Jesus' 2 Cor 4:10) it is really he who is giving himself again through us. He can only live through us one kind and quality of life, and that is his own! Besides the anticipated love, purity, patience and other fruit of the Spirit, there is the overriding sacrificial self-giving. If that element is missing (seen or hidden), then what we have is but the human image of God. That can be wonderful, of course, but spiritually it is dead since the Fall.

In the death and resurrection of our spiritual experience, there is not only this fuller life for us, but also life for others just as it was for him and us in the once and for all sacrifice of Calvary.

And that is what it is all about, isn't it?

22

And Now Forward?

And so, what now? It is not necessary to agree with all the ideas put forward in the preceding pages. But one thing is certain. No spiritually alive person is going to claim that they have no need of knowing God in a deeper way. Further, we can see clearly that that knowledge comes by means of revelation. It started that way and will only continue in the same way. For some there is a touch of desperation in the realisation that not only is our meaningful service involved in this advance, but something which might be called the quality of our life in eternity is at issue.

Revelation comes in the process of 'rest'—that is another certainty. But as normal men and women, how can we find the time for this rest? There is the everyday occupation of just living! Business; the family; running a house; friends; travelling; relaxation; Christian service; in this activity-orientated society, you name it, and I've got whatever it takes to prevent my getting quiet with God.

It sounds simplistic, but the result of many counselling sessions shows that the issue turns on the reality of my desire to fulfil God's will. This desire can be measured by the depth of our understanding of the death of Christ. 'He died for me' is very easily said! The time comes when to go forward involves a certain amount of sacrifice; some degree of inconvenience; some interruption to what is normally our legitimate way of life. But somehow, surely, we must get off this roundabout of human living, which is just a passing thing, and find our way into eternal reality. What does God want to accomplish through me to 'serve my day and generation'? It may be to sweep roads or evangelise a nation. I need to be sure (live by faith) and that he is doing the work through me. My way of living may change a little or dramatically or not at all. But it will issue from the spiritual reality of my union with Christ, and therefore will be life-giving in the love of God and in the way he chooses.

Somehow we must make time. What is meant is that having all the time that God grants the human race, we must organise our use of it appropriately. Further, God is not to be switched on and off, and therefore much depends on how much we have already seen to it that we have a conscious fellowship with him. What some people call 'the old fashioned quiet time' is hard to beat to engender this. Come to think of it, what becomes of the relationship with someone we love if we do not take the time to be with them, and them alone, as much as is practicable? And we love God?

There is no better time for this communion of thought, prayer for others, and Bible reading, than first thing in the morning. Even when young children are around this is possible normally if we start early enough! Early enough? Cut some of the telly, go to bed earlier, and use an alarm clock if necessary. How long we spend on this can vary, obviously, and may well call for the co-operation of a family partner. But we do it in order to prepare the way for entry into the Fifth Dimension. Any Christian bookshop will offer useful Bible reading notes and other helpful devotional material. The needs of friends, named missionaries, world and national news, can all provide subjects for prayer for others.

It is out of such a practical prayer life that the vista of the Fifth Dimension can be seen at least dimly. Can we accept the initial bother, inconvenience, 'sacrifice'? If not, we may as well give up, because God is not an optional extra any more than a husband is to a wife, or a wife to a husband, once the relationship is established. To climb a ladder it is no good trying to leap straight onto the tenth rung!

Now we know at least something of fellowship with our Father. Now we have a concern to serve him. And now we must somehow spend time to allow him to reveal himself, the I AM; to reveal who we are as one in union with him; to show us his way for the creative activity of the New Creation through which he works; to become 'co-labourers with God', to 'take his yoke on us', to work with him and not just for him. 'Gold, silver and precious stones' and not just 'wood, hay and stubble'.

The problem of finding an extended time when we can be alone with God will be something to wrestle with firmly. It will have to be repeated. In any case, from time to time, in the face of some issue, we shall always find it 'easier' to do if we have once before succeeded. Experience suggests that at least a full day is desirable. This may well have to be a Sunday, and our first break away may have to be in the religious realm and with some misunderstanding in anyone who knows what we do! You may decide to miss a meal, with something to drink at the psychological pressure points of meal times.

Such a move is easy enough for a single person, or a married couple without children. But what about the parents with a family? The following arrangement has been found workable and profitable.

One parent—generally mother—takes over the children from the beginning of their day. Missing the meal herself perhaps, she prepares breakfast and lunch for them, and generally looks after them until after lunch. Meanwhile, father is at prayer (and about that and similar matters, more later). After lunch, father takes over the children, sees them to their afternoon or evening meal and gets them to bed. Mother meanwhile is at prayer. Once the children are in bed and ministered to appropriately by mother, father or both, the parents can continue together after sharing anything the Lord has spoken about. Later evening, there can be a sharing before final prayer.

You may be considering including your children, but the depth of experience I have in mind makes it inappropriate. This is not a family prayer day (good though that is); this is as it were an ascent to Sinai's peak, which made even Moses tremble!

The above merely outlines how time can be found, and other methods can come to mind. The question always is: How much do we want to find that time? Find it, and we can begin to find 'rest' and be prepared for revelation.

How we use that time we can suggest in the following chapter.

23

An Outline of Action

It is difficult for some people to imagine how they can use up a whole day (or longer) thinking, reading and praying 'before the Lord'. Therefore in the context of the last chapter, and leading on from it, the following suggestions are given. Eventually, it is the Holy Spirit who will guide, of course. But the ideas now shared arise from experience and therefore may be of use to some one. If my grandmother happens to read this, I hope she will forgive my teaching her to suck eggs!

Try to find a place that really will be quiet. In the normal household this will generally be a bedroom. Make sure everyone else in the house will leave you alone, and that phone callers will be told that you are not available. Place the Bible, any devotional book, paper and pencil and anything else you think of on the bed. Kneel at the bedside. It is true that one can commune with God in any physical position; in fact, some may not be able to kneel. However, the kneeling position does seem helpful, at least to start with. But be comfortable—use a cushion to kneel on! Discomfort can be distracting. If nevertheless this does occur, sit up somewhere for a while, or even walk about in the room. Finally, if at some point you doze, don't worry! After all, you are seeking at first complete inner rest, and physical relaxation is at least a good preparation if we have never yet known that rest. Later, the Spirit will seal this inner rest in a wonderful way, and then all the external turmoil will not disturb it.

Do not start praying about anything or anybody, even yourself. Deliberately stop thinking about people, work, and especially the Christian service in which you are involved normally. Seek merely to concentrate on the fact that God is, and that he is there with you. Paul says that it is in him that we live, and move and have our being. (Acts 17:28). This will lead to uncluttered worship, when you can express your gratitude for his love and the fact that he has given you new life in Christ. Certainly don't worry about the form of words. Speak with him; tell him, in 'private audience'. But do not start asking for things or experiences.

Clearly, one must have a 'listening heart' at all times, and especially when just resting in his presence. Read a little, perhaps from the devotional book, or if the Bible, begin with the Pauline epistles. Be ready to stop and pray in response to anything that 'touches' you; this will probably be in thanksgiving or a request to 'make that real for me'. Do not hurry—feed, even if this part of the day takes several hours.

But through all this time there will begin to rise a desire to open one's heart to the Lord's searching and possible cleansing. There will be no sense of abandonment in the rest of his love, when nothing else but him matters much. Remember the word of the writer to the Hebrews: 'Strive, labour, seek, to enter into this rest' (Heb 4:11) for we can be sure that 'There remains a rest to the people of God' (Heb 4:9). Read the whole chapter and on the basis of verse thirteen, ask to be shown anything that is less than the best in:

Relationships, family and otherwise.
Practices at daily work.
Attitudes to people of other races;
    other political ideas; other religions.
Pe sonal reactions (eg bad temper; lust;
    critical spirit; and others.)
Finance and possessions.
Habits.
Slackness concerning maintaining my fellowship with
    God and his people.
Anything else which in your heart of
    hearts, the Holy Spirit shows to be wrong.

Then lay hold on verses 14 to 16 of Hebrews 4 and meditate on the truth of 1 John 1:6–9. Then praise God for his faithfulness—you can do little else!

This, once more, may well take more time than we think at first. Don't be casual; God can do more with a bad reality than he can with a false righteousness!

We should by this time be able to see to what extent our life's activities, including our so-called Christian service, are based on our personal desires or our own talents and abilities, our best-intentioned self efforts. In effect, to be able to detect what is not in fact by faith. Now, hurt though it may, argue though we may, we must look at the end phrase of Romans chapter 14 and verse 23. 'What is not of faith is sin'.

Sin. But the Lord Jesus died to deliver us and to cleanse us from that! So there is no condemnation! Can you praise the Lord for that and just accept the fact because he says so? We need never know anything but complete freedom from now on.

You may even wish to read a part of this book again! Or if it is still fairly clear in your mind, lay before the Lord all the relevant activities you are normally engaged in. Does he witness to your Spirit that he will work through them? Does he say that they are a part of the yoke he is wearing? You will be willing to let things go or take up something else. Nothing matters, so long as he does the work through things you normally can do or things that are normally beyond you. You are at rest, and the revelation of his working is yours out from the Fifth Dimension. Go in the good of that knowledge, and trust him to be working it out as you resolutely refuse to be activity-orientated again. 'Looking away to Jesus' (Heb 12:2)—you may see many things and people, but you can only look at one thing or person at a time. 'Looking' is a concentration of 'seeing'. 'Looking' like this is faith.

A Prayer

O Lord, my God, my Father God, the I AM,
   who inhabits eternity beyond my understanding,

   please confirm by the witness of your Spirit with
   mine that I am indeed your spiritual child
   through faith in the redeeming work of the Lord
   Jesus Christ on the cross;

   reveal to me more of the cost of that redemption
   so that I may have no hesitation in abandoning
   myself, and what I am and have, to the will of
   your love;

   teach me to rest completely within my own self
   with the expectation of the Holy Spirit revealing
   you to be living in me;

   show me through the reading of your word more
   and more of the resources at our disposal (you
   and I) to enable the needs of a lost mankind to be
   met in some effective way through me;

keep my vision of your resurrection Self within me and around me to thwart the efforts of your enemy, Satan.

with your courage and faith I will respond to what you show me in the quietness of eternity in my own heart. Teach me to recognise the beginning of any self-effort, even to serve you, and cleanse me from such 'dead works' of the past;

I ask for all this, and more as you prompt me, because as your new creation, anything less would deny Calvary and keep me from the rest in union with yourself which you have given, and out of which I shall begin to see your purpose through me to fulfil your will.

Amen.

Bibliography

The following is just a short list of books which could be found helpful as background reading or for use during times of 'resting'.

A visit to a Christian bookshop can be an introduction to various aids to daily Bible reading. Among these are Scripture Union's *Daily Notes* and Crusade for World Revival's *Every Day With Jesus* notes. An assistant can generally give advice as to the degree of advanced study.

The first four books mentioned below can also be used in daily devotions. There are, of course, many others.

Osward Chambers *My Utmost for His Highest*, Marshall Morgan & Scott, 1972

Amy Carmichael *If*, Triangle, 1987, and also *His Thoughts Said*, Dohnavur Books, 1941

Norman Grubb *Summit Living*, Christian Literature Crusade, USA, 1987

Judson Cornwall *Unfeigned Faith*, Kingsway, 1985

Philip Elston *Travelling On*, Angel Press, 1986

David Watson *Discipleship*, Hodder & Stoughton, 1983

Andrew Murray *Waiting on God*, Lakeland Publications, 1968

Elisabeth Elliot *Amy Carmichael: Her Life and Legacy*, Kingsway, 1988

Joyce Huggett *Listening to God*, Hodder & Stoughton, 1986

J I Packer *Knowing God*, Hodder & Stoughton, 1975

Dick Dowsett *God, That's Not Fair!*, OMF Books, 1982

Martin Goldsmith *Don't Just Stand There*, IVP, 1976

It is good to choose such books prayerfully. Different ones appeal to different people. Most of the authors have written other books which can be equally helpful.

Bible Meditation

by Alex Buchanan

A life centred on God—an elusive dream, or a daily reality?

Alex Buchanan believes that it is possible to know the peace, guidance and joy of God's presence day by day. We in the West starve ourselves when we have an ample supply of food all around us—God's written word.

This book shows that meditating on Scripture can be one of life's most rewarding and exciting experiences, opening the door to heavenly riches—as long as we refuse to adopt the world's get-rich-quick mentality. More than that, we see how Spirit-filled prophecy and an effective prayer life flow out of the new dimension that Bible meditation brings to those who won't settle for anything less.

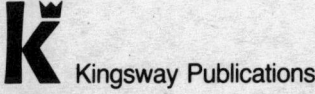

Kingsway Publications

Knowing God's Will

by Paul Miller

Christians believe that God has revealed his will to men and women down the ages. The Bible is prized as a perfect and fully sufficient record of his dealings with mankind, containing everything we need to know about his will for us in general.

But how do I check out with God my own personal decisions? Is 'sanctified common sense' enough?

What place should I give to the advice of others, and to 'words from the Lord' given in good faith?

How do I know it is God's voice I am hearing, especially when things don't turn out the way I thought he meant them to?

'This is a book that will answer these questions, and many more! I highly recommend it to you.'
—Floyd McClung, Executive Director, International Operations, Youth With A Mission

Paul Miller is the Director of Youth With A Mission in London.

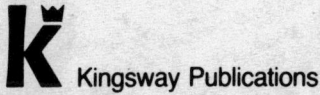

Kingsway Publications

Pray in the Spirit

by Arthur Wallis

In this book Arthur Wallis concentrates on the ministry of the Holy Spirit in relation to prayer, and investigates the full meaning of the apostle's injunction to 'pray in the Spirit'.

He analyses the spiritual and practical difficulties we encounter, and shows how the Holy Spirit helps us in our weakness and makes up for all our deficiencies. We are encouraged to yield ourselves completely to Him, allowing Him to pray through us.

As we enter into the 'deep things of God' unfolded here we shall discover a new power and effectiveness in our Christian lives.

Kingsway Publications